MW01114442

AN INTRODUCTION TO THE FELONY COURT SYSTEM IN VIRGINIA

BY JENNIFER RAIMO

Copyright © 2015 by Jennifer Raimo

All rights reserved. No part of this book may be used or reproduced in any manner whatsoever without written permission of the author.

DISCLAIMER: THIS BOOK IS MEANT FOR GENERAL INFORMATIONAL PURPOSES ONLY AND IS NOT INTENDED AS LEGAL ADVICE. Each person's individual situation is different. Before taking any legal action, it is highly recommended that you consult with an attorney in your area concerning your specific cicumstances.

Printed in the United States of America

ISBN: 978-1-63385-066-8

Design and publishing by:
Word Association Publishers
205 Fifth Avenue
Tarentum, Pennsylvania 15084

www.wordassociation.com
1.800.827.7903

CONTENT

INTRODUCTION

This book is meant to be a guide to help people who are facing felony charges to understand how the court system works. It can also be useful to people who want to understand what a friend or family member goes through when facing a felony charge. We will be reviewing the steps of a felony court case from arrest through trial and sentencing hearings.

I represent people every day who have been accused of some type of crime. I've written this book because I've noticed that some of my clients get nervous before court hearings and forget what to expect in court. I hope this book will serve as an easy reference for people to remind themselves of what to expect from the criminal justice system and to keep their stress level at a minimum during the months a court case may be pending.

This book is intended to present general information only and should not be considered legal advice or create an attorney-client relationship. I will not discuss defense strategies in this book or what must be proven in order to be convicted of any specific crime. No book can do a good job of addressing the unique facts and circumstances of any given case. Anyone who is facing felony charges should seek advice from a competent attorney in a confidential environment.

MEET JOE AND SHEILA

Joe and Sheila are facing felony charges in northern Virginia. Throughout this book, we will be following their cases at each stage of the court's proceedings. These people are purely fictional, and any resemblance to real life is purely coincidental.

Joe and Sheila have been happily married for six years. Joe had court last October for drunk driving. He was found guilty, and his driver's license was suspended for 12 months. In addition, he was given a suspended jail sentence and a fine, and was ordered to complete an alcohol safety action class. Sheila does not have a criminal record.

Last Friday, Joe lost his ride to work and decided to borrow Sheila's car. On the way to work, a car crossed over the double yellow line into Joe's lane of travel and crashed into Joe's car. Joe looked inside the other car and knew the woman inside must be seriously injured because she was staring at nothing in particular and would not speak or look at him. Joe called 911 to request an ambulance. Then he remembered his lawyer had told him he could go to jail if he was caught driving while his license was suspended, and he got scared. Joe ran home and took the day off from work. The other driver died sometime before an ambulance arrived at the scene of the accident.

CHAPTER 1

WARRANT/ARREST

Most felony cases start with an arrest warrant and an arrest. Depending on the circumstances of an individual case, it is possible for a person to be arrested before or after an arrest warrant is issued. In Virginia, the police do not have to have a perfect case in order to arrest a suspect. All that is needed at this stage is probable cause to believe the suspect has committed the crime that he is being accused of committing. Once an arrest warrant is issued for most crimes, the accused cannot avoid being arrested.[1] He should hire a lawyer to help him turn himself in as soon as possible for the best chance of being allowed to have a bail bond.

Sometimes a person gets tricked into committing

---

1 A judge can withdraw an arrest warrant for failure to appear for a court hearing if a motion is filed and scheduled for hearing. A lawyer can help get this type of motion on the docket quickly and explain the reason for the defendant's absence in the best possible light.

a crime with someone else. It happens most often to people who are charged with receiving stolen property or obtaining property or money under false pretenses, but I've also seen it happen in forgery, bad check, and credit card fraud cases. Usually the person learns she has committed a crime when a police officer comes to arrest her.

In many cases like this, the police will want to interrogate the accused before he has a chance to get a lawyer. They do it now because they know a good lawyer will tell the accused not to waive any rights or speak to the police. They might "read him his rights" and then downplay how serious those rights are. The accused should refuse to waive any rights. He can always choose to speak with the police later if his lawyer believes it is good for trial strategy. However, I cannot recall a time in my career when I've advised someone to speak with the police after they've been arrested. Once an arrest has been made, the police are only interested in getting a conviction and not in helping the accused. For more information about the right to remain silent, see the section "A Note about the Miranda Warnings" below.

Sometimes the person realizes she has been asked to commit a crime before the police find out about it. The person should never ignore it when she realizes the plan is illegal, because the police will eventually look to arrest and prosecute her. In those cases, it may be possible to avoid getting arrested if the person comes forward quickly and helps the police with their investigation. The person should be prepared to testify against the mastermind who tricked her or asked her to commit a crime. It is best to have a lawyer approach the police first so you can remain anonymous while the lawyer works to keep police interest in arresting the innocent accomplice at a minimum or even get a promise not to prosecute in exchange for helping the police.

A NOTE ABOUT THE MIRANDA WARNINGS

One of the most common questions I hear from people

who are accused of a felony is whether the case can be dismissed because the police never "read me my rights." Ever since the famous case of *Miranda v. Arizona* was decided by the United States Supreme Court, Hollywood has done an excellent job of teaching Americans about rights that are guaranteed to all criminal defendants. Unfortunately, Hollywood has been equally successful about misinforming people as to when those rights must be read to a suspect. The short answer to the question is to say that "reading rights" is not a part of the arrest process. The fact that a person's rights were not read to him will not help the accused in most cases.

Miranda v. Arizona requires police officers to advise a suspect or criminal defendant of certain rights before beginning a *custodial interrogation*. There are four such warnings: (1) the suspect has the right to remain silent; (2) anything the suspect says can and will be used against him; (3) the suspect has the right to have an attorney present during questioning; and (4) if the suspect cannot afford to

have an attorney, one will be appointed to represent him.
[2] If a police officer interrogates (or as they prefer to say "interviews") a suspect before arresting him, the officer does not normally have to read the Miranda warnings, because the accused is not in custody. Likewise, if a person is arrested and starts sharing information about the crime with a police officer on his own without being asked about the crime, the statement(s) can be used against the accused in court because, although he was in custody, he was not being interrogated when that information was revealed.

A surefire way to be convicted of a crime is to agree to speak with the police about a crime they believe you have committed, regardless of whether or not they read you your rights. Despite the language of the Miranda warnings, which strongly implies the police are not interested in helping the suspect, most criminal defendants find themselves being arrested *after* having waived their

---

2 384 U.S. 436 (1966).

rights and being interrogated, sometimes for hours.

If you are ever asked by a police officer to speak about a crime you are suspected of having committed, you should refuse to do so, no matter how much pressure you may feel to do what the officer wants and no matter how many times a police officer asks for the "interview." It may not be good enough to just say no or remain silent.[3] Instead, you should say you are exercising your constitutional right to remain silent unless a lawyer is present during the "interview" to help you, and add that you will not waive any of your constitutional rights.

Be prepared to feel accused, dirty, and bad about yourself. Not many officers will take no for an answer on the first try. Instead, they say things like, "If you don't

---

3   The United States Supreme Court decided in 2013 that there are some circumstances where remaining silent can be interpreted by the police as an admission of guilty and used against the accused in court unless the accused specifically tells the police he is exercising his constitutional right to remain silent. *Salinas v. Texas*, 133 S. Ct. 2174.

answer my questions, that means you're guilty," or "You must be a bad person," or "The other person told us the truth, so why don't you just admit it's true? They don't have a reason to lie, do they?" Another common police strategy is to call the crime a mistake and suggest they can do something to help you instead of arresting you. The truth is no police officer has any intention of doing anything to help you correct a mistake without first getting a criminal conviction and court order for the help as a condition of probation. Finally, if the officer has read you your rights, you may hear him appeal to your sense of curiosity by telling you he cannot tell you what the case is about unless you first waive your rights and agree to speak with him. They follow up that statement by asking you, "Don't you want to know what this is all about?" You'll find out soon enough through your lawyer and the court system what it is all about. A good lawyer will be able to protect your rights every step of the way.

The bottom line is you have the right to remain

silent, and anything you say can and will be used against you. If you hear those words being spoken to you by a police officer, he means it. Anything you say can and will be used against you, even if it means using the words to tell the prosecutor, judge, and jury you were expressing something you never meant to say. You need to tell the police you are exercising your right to remain silent until a lawyer can be present to help you, and then stand your ground and remain silent.

INVESTIGATION AND ARREST
OF JOE AND SHEILA

As I mentioned in the introduction, Joe was involved in a car accident and ran away from the scene. Officer Smith used the license plate to trace the car back to Joe's wife, Sheila. He went to Joe and Sheila's house to question Sheila about the accident later in the day. Sheila had taken the metro train to work that day and was not home. Joe did not answer the door when Officer Smith rang the doorbell.

Officer Smith returned to Joe and Sheila's house on Saturday morning. Sheila answered the door and agreed to discuss what she knew about the accident with him. Officer Smith did not read Sheila's rights, and Sheila did not think to ask if she had to speak to him. Sheila said Joe had used her car to go to work because the family depends on his income to pay the bills and he didn't have a ride. She knew Joe had been in an accident and totaled the car, but Joe was going to be okay. As far as Sheila knew, Joe had already called the insurance and was taking care of everything.

Officer Smith thanked Sheila for the information. He told Sheila he would have to discuss what happened with his boss, and he left. Then he went to the local magistrate and requested arrest warrants for Joe for driving while revoked,[4] and felony hit and run.[5] At the same time, he

---

4 Virginia Code § 18.2-272.
5 Virginia Code § 46.2-894.

requested a warrant for Sheila for the misdemeanor of allowing a person with no legal right to drive.[6] Joe's warrants required that he be arrested. Sheila, however, was allowed to be released on a summons, meaning she could be given a ticket instead of being arrested. Joe and Sheila were not told about the arrest warrants.

Officer Smith returned to Joe and Sheila's home on February 1 to serve the warrants just as they were pulling into the driveway in a rental car. Sheila signed an acknowledgement of her charge and court date without incident. When Joe was asked to step out of the car, he knew he was about to be arrested, and he was overcome with fear. Joe had never been to jail before and did not want to go now. He picked up Sheila's purse as he stepped out of the car and used it to hit Officer Smith in the face with all his strength. The purse broke open and a small bag

---

6 Virginia Code § 46.2-349.

of cocaine fell onto the driveway. Joe started to run away but was tackled by a few officers before he got to the end of the driveway.

Officer Jones was one of the officers who tackled Joe. When it became clear that Joe would not be able to get away and Officer Smith had Joe under control, Officer Jones decided to investigate the bag of powder that had fallen out of Sheila's purse. He did not read Sheila her rights, but instead asked what was in the bag. She tried to convince Officer Jones the bag was nothing special. Officer Jones told her she was making things worse for herself and that she should just admit she had cocaine. She refused to admit any such thing. Officer Jones told her he would call a drug dog to sniff Sheila and he would arrest her if she didn't admit it now. She pulled another baggie out of her pocket and asked Officer Jones not to do anything to her. The powder is cocaine. She is the owner and is addicted to it. Joe knows she uses cocaine and where she keeps it. Sometimes he helps himself to her stash when he needs a little "pick-me-up." Then Officer Jones arrested Sheila and charged her with possession of cocaine.[7]

Joe found himself to be in a more difficult situation. In addition to being arrested for driving while revoked and for hit and run, Joe was charged with possession of cocaine,[8] assault and battery of a law enforcement officer,[9] and resisting arrest.[10]

Officer Smith drove Joe to the local adult detention center. On the way, Joe apologized for having hit him. Joe said he just did it because he was scared and didn't want to go to jail. Officer Smith advised Joe of his rights: (1) he had the right to remain silent, (2) anything he said could be used against him, (3) he had the right to have an attorney present during questioning, and (4) he had the right to have an attorney appointed if he could not afford one.

---

7 Virginia Code § 18.2-250.

8 Virginia Code § 18.2-250.

9 Virginia Code § 18.2-57(C).

10 Virginia Code § 18.2-479.1.

Officer Smith then asked Joe why he would have been scared about going to jail. Joe explained to Officer Smith the reason why he had decided to drive to work, how the accident had happened, and that he had not asked Sheila before taking the car. When confronted with the death of the other driver, Joe was very upset and told Officer Smith the other driver was alive and that Joe had called an ambulance before he ran away.

CHAPTER 2

BOND DETERMINATION BY THE MAGISTRATE

When a person is arrested, she is taken to the local magistrate's office. The accused will be advised of the charge(s), and the magistrate will make a decision whether or not to grant a bond. There are several types of bonds. All of them require the accused to sign a written promise to appear in court for all hearings and comply with any special conditions that may be imposed while the case is pending. Common examples of special conditions are orders not to leave the state or contact the alleged victim and orders for pretrial supervision by a probation officer.

The magistrate has several options. First, he can choose to allow an unsecured bond (commonly called a personal recognizance), meaning the accused may leave the jail by promising to come to all court hearings and pay money to the court if she breaks the promise to be there. Second, the magistrate can decide to allow a cash bond, meaning the accused or someone acting on her behalf must pay a certain amount of cash money directly to the magistrate's office before the accused will be allowed to leave the local jail. The money would either be refunded at the end of the case if the accused attends all court hearings or be lost forever if the accused fails to appear at any hearing. This is the least common type of bond. Third, the magistrate may authorize a secured cash / corporate surety bond, meaning the accused can choose to either pay the full bond in cash to the magistrate or hire a bail bondsman to pay the bond for a lesser fee, usually 10 percent of the amount of the bond. Finally, the magistrate may decide not to authorize a bond, meaning the accused will be detained in the local jail until trial or until a judge is persuaded to modify the magistrate's decision.

Some types of violent cases or "repeat-offender" cases have a presumption against bond. In those cases, a magistrate is not authorized to grant bond. However, bond can still be granted by a general district court, juvenile and domestic relations court, or circuit court judge as soon as a day or two following the arrest if the accused's attorney can convince a judge that the presumption against bond should not apply in a particular case.[11] Some examples of a presumed no-bond charge are murder, malicious wounding, possession of a firearm after being convicted of a felony, and a third or subsequent offense of domestic assault.[12] Illegal immigrants may have trouble convincing a judge to authorize a bond if United States Immigration and Customs Enforcement ("ICE") issues a detainer to begin removal proceedings.[13]

JOE AND SHEILA'S BOND DETERMINATION BY THE MAGISTRATE

Joe arrived at the adult detention center first and was taken to see the magistrate. The magistrate did not

---

11 See chapter 4 for more information about bond motions in court.

12 Virginia Code § 19.2-120.

13 Virginia Code § 19.2-120.1.

grant Joe a bond and told him he would have to go to jail.

Sheila was taken to the magistrate soon after Joe. Officer Jones told the magistrate Sheila had been polite and cooperative with him but also had cocaine in her possession. The magistrate granted Sheila a $2,000 bond and told her she could pay the full $2,000 in cash to the magistrate and get that money back at the end of the case or she could hire a bail bondsman to pay the bond for her. Sheila called her brother to ask him to pay the full bond to the magistrate, and she reimbursed him from her savings account. She had to spend about four hours in the adult detention center's receiving area before her bond was paid and processed.

CHAPTER 3

ARRAIGNMENT/APPOINTMENT OF COUNSEL

Shortly after an arrest, the accused is expected to appear in court for an arraignment hearing. If the accused is in jail, the arraignment is usually on the first business day after the arrest. If the accused is able to pay a bond on the day of the arrest, the arraignment tends to be about one week later.

At an arraignment, a judge will tell the accused the name of the charge(s) and inform the accused that the charge is one that carries the possibility of a jail sentence. The accused has a right to have an attorney represent him in court and the right to have one appointed if he cannot afford one. The judge will ask the accused whether he intends to hire a lawyer or if he wants to be interviewed to determine whether he qualifies to have a public defender or court-appointed attorney represent him. Only people who cannot afford to hire an attorney according to state standards and people who are held in jail without bond qualify to have an attorney appointed for them.

At this stage of the proceedings, the judge will not ask anyone how they plead and will not want to hear any evidence. Although judges may consider granting bond at this stage for people who are being held in jail, it is not often done. Because the purpose of this hearing is to advise defendants of the right to counsel and appoint counsel quickly for people who cannot afford an attorney, a prosecutor may or may not be present at the arraignment.

JOE'S ARRAIGNMENT

On Monday morning (two days after the arrest), Joe was taken to a room with a video camera. He saw a judge on television and could talk to the judge through the television. The judge told Joe what his charges were and advised him that, because the charges have a possible prison sentence, he had the right to have an attorney appointed if he could not afford one. Joe said he would prefer to hire a lawyer and did not want to be interviewed for court-appointed counsel. The judge was reluctant to accept Joe's answer. He postponed the arraignment two days to review the status of Joe's search for an attorney and to consider appointing counsel if Joe still did not have a lawyer.

SHEILA'S ARRAIGNMENT

About one week after her arrest, Sheila had her first court hearing. She was nervous about it because she had not yet been able to find a lawyer to help her and was not sure if she should plead guilty or not guilty. Before the judge started calling names, he made some introductory comments to everyone present in the courtroom. The judge explained that everyone who had a court case on the docket for that courtroom at that time of day was here because they have been charged with a crime for which they could go to jail. Because of that, they have the right to have a lawyer help them in court. Anyone who believed they could not afford to hire a lawyer could request to be interviewed for court-appointed counsel. The court will only appoint counsel for people whose income is close to or below the poverty line.

When the judge called Sheila's name, Sheila told the judge she wanted to be interviewed for court-appointed counsel. A clerk asked Sheila how much money she earns and how much she pays for rent, car payments, medical bills, and other expenses. Then Sheila raised her right hand and swore under penalty of law that the answers she had given to the clerk were true and accurate.

The clerk gave Sheila's paperwork to the judge, and Sheila waited for the judge to review it and call her name again. When the judge called Sheila's name, he told her that even though she had already spent more money than she would have liked, Sheila's income was too high to qualify for court-appointed counsel.

CHAPTER 4

BOND MOTIONS IN COURT AND CONDITIONS OF BOND

If a magistrate does not grant bond to a defendant or the bond is too expensive for a defendant to pay, it is possible to file a bond motion in the general district or juvenile and domestic relations court where the arraignment was heard. The bond motion is filed by an attorney in advance of the date the motion will be on the court's docket. The local rules about how far in advance the motion should be filed vary from court to court.

On the day of the bond motion, the defense attorney will usually tell the judge what the evidence would be if anyone were to testify, and argue for a reasonable bond to be granted. In some cases, the lawyer will need to formally present evidence. The prosecutor will also have an opportunity to discuss evidence and present an argument representing the state's position on the issue. The judge will decide whether to grant a reduced bond and may order any special requirements as the judge believes appropriate under the circumstances.

If bond is still denied by the general district court or juvenile and domestic relations court judge, the accused can appeal that decision to the local circuit court. A circuit court judge usually hears the bond motion on a different day and makes her own decision as to bond based on the evidence and argument that is presented in the circuit court on the day of the motion. Nothing that happened in the lower court is considered unless it is re-presented in the circuit court. It is as though nothing happened in the lower court.

If a circuit court judge does not grant bond, a defendant has the right to have that decision reviewed by the Virginia Court of Appeals. Such an appeal would have to be made in writing and sent to the Court of Appeals in Richmond, Virginia. This is not a new bond motion, but merely a review of the judge's decision to determine whether the circuit court judge's decision was unreasonable. Appealing a bond decision to the Court of Appeals is usually unsuccessful for the defendant.

A NOTE ABOUT BOND CONDITIONS

Any magistrate or judge who grants a bail bond may impose restrictions on the accused. The most common restrictions are an order not to leave the state, not to have any contact with an alleged victim, not to return to the location where the crime is alleged to have occurred, or to be supervised by a probation officer while awaiting trial. Other restrictions or special conditions of bond may be required as the magistrate or judge deems appropriate for a specific case.

JOE'S BOND MOTIONS IN COURT

On Tuesday afternoon (three days after his arrest), Joe's lawyer filed two documents in court: a praecipe[14]

---

14 A praecipe can best be described as a note to the clerk. This type of document is often used by attorneys to notify the court who will be representing the accused in a criminal case or as a cover sheet asking the clerk to schedule a motion (request for the judge to consider) for a certain day.

telling the clerk she would be the defense attorney for Joe's case and a bond motion, which was scheduled to be heard on Wednesday. On Wednesday, Joe's lawyer was able to convince a general district court judge that Joe had many reasons to stay in the local area, that he would come to court for all hearings, and that he would not be a danger to the community if he were granted bond. The general district court judge granted Joe a $50,000 cash or corporate surety bond for all of the charges combined. Like Sheila, Joe had the choice of paying the full amount of the bond to the magistrate or hiring a bail bondsman for about 10 percent of that amount.

Joe asked Sheila to hire a bail bondsman, but the bond was too expensive for Sheila to pay, even by hiring a bail bondsman. So Joe asked his lawyer to appeal the bond to the circuit court. The new bond motion could not be heard in circuit court until the beginning of the following week.

In circuit court, Joe's lawyer was able to convince

the judge to lower Joe's bond to $5,000 cash or corporate surety, but the judge also ordered: (1) Joe would have to participate in a form of probation before trial, commonly called pretrial supervision; (2) Joe would not be allowed to leave the state of Virginia; and (3) someone would have to give Joe's passport to the magistrate before Joe would be allowed to leave the jail.

Sheila was able to pay $625 (10 percent of the bond amount plus a $125 administrative fee) and give Joe's passport to a bail bondsman so Joe could come home. The bail bondsman explained to Sheila the $625 was a fee for the bondsman's services and is nonrefundable. No matter what happens in the case, the fee will not be refunded (even if Joe is found not guilty). Sheila also had to sign a contract with the bondsman's business in which she agreed she would be personally responsible for reimbursing the bondsman the full $5,000 bond if Joe were to miss any of his court hearings and have his bond surrendered. By the time Sheila was able to make the arrangements for Joe to come home, he had spent a total of eight days in jail.

JOE'S PRETRIAL SUPERVISION VIOLATION

As conditions of his bond, Joe was not allowed to leave the state of Virginia and was required to submit to pretrial supervision. When Joe was released on bond, the magistrate at the jail told him he was required to report to the court services office on the next business day. Joe was given the address and telephone number so he could easily schedule his first appointment.

Joe was so stressed out about the events of the past week that the magistrate's words went over his head. He signed the bond recognizance form and left.

Joe did not look at the paperwork he received from the jail for at least two weeks. He read he should have already reported to court services, and he felt a sense of panic rising up inside him. He called court services and scheduled an appointment for the next day.

When he arrived at the appointment, Joe learned that court services considered him to be in violation of pretrial supervision because he was late in scheduling his appointment, but the probation officer had decided to give him a warning instead of asking a judge to revoke his bond right away.

The probation officer then told Joe some rules he would have to obey. Joe was given a schedule of in-person appointments and telephone appointments. All of the appointments were during normal business hours, often in the middle of the day. Joe responded that the appointments were too frequent and at bad times because they were during his work hours, but the probation officer did not care. Joe's choices were to accept the appointments or go back to jail.

The probation officer also told Joe he was not allowed to drink alcohol or use illegal drugs. To prove he was clean, Joe would have to submit to random drug screening while his case was pending. Joe was especially upset about this because he had been using marijuana and cocaine since the alcohol safety class for his drunk driving conviction ended. He knew he did not have a problem, and he did not want someone to tell him what he could and could not do. The probation officer reminded Joe he did not have a choice in the matter and required Joe to submit to a drug test before leaving the office.

Joe took the test. It came back positive for both marijuana and cocaine. At Joe's next appointment, his probation officer told him he would have to participate in treatment for drug addiction. Joe said he would do it but decided not to accept any treatment or meet with his probation officer ever again. He moved in with his son and daughter-in-law in Delaware and decided he would never return to Virginia again.

The probation officer sent a letter to the judge stating that Joe had not complied with pretrial supervision by delaying in scheduling his first appointment, testing positive for marijuana and cocaine, refusing to comply with drug treatment, failing to call in for telephone appointments, and failing to appear for in-person appointments.

Upon receiving the probation officer's letter, the judge issued a rule to show cause why Joe's bond should not be revoked, and he scheduled a hearing. Joe did not come to court on the day of the hearing, and the judge issued a warrant for Joe's arrest.

In addition to breaking the rules of the supervised release program, Joe missed his preliminary hearing (discussed in chapter 6). After the new arrest warrant was served on him, he would have to face an additional charge of failure to appear.

JOE'S OUT-OF-STATE ARREST AND EXTRADITION

Two months later, Joe got in an argument outside of a bar in Delaware and was arrested for being drunk in public and for the failure to appear in Virginia. Joe went to jail to wait for a judge to decide whether to send him back to Virginia for trial.

The next morning, Joe had a short hearing in Delaware where the judge told him he was accused of failure to appear in a Virginia court. Joe had two choices: (1) wait in jail until an extradition hearing could be scheduled for him to dispute Virginia's right to extradite him (come get Joe and take him back to Virginia for trial), or (2) waive an extradition hearing and wait in jail for Virginia to come get him. Regardless of what Joe decided, he was not going to be allowed to have a bail bond that day. Joe decided to waive an extradition hearing because it would be the fastest way to get out of jail.

A few days later, two sheriff deputies arrived at the Delaware jail to take Joe back to Virginia. When he arrived in Virginia, the magistrate ordered that Joe be held without bond in the local adult detention center until his lawyer could file a bond motion.

JOE'S ARRAIGNMENT AND BOND MOTIONS FOR FAILURE TO APPEAR

The morning after Joe arrived in Virginia, he had an arraignment hearing in general district court. The judge informed Joe he was charged with failure to appear for his preliminary hearing. The judge told Joe his lawyer would be contacted and informed that Joe had been found. Joe was also advised of the new date scheduled for a preliminary hearing. Joe had to remain in the adult detention center without bond.

Joe's lawyer came to the detention center to visit him and discuss whether it would be best to file a bond motion. Joe hated being locked up and desperately wanted a bond motion, even though he had broken the rules of pretrial supervision and had also left the state without permission.

Joe's lawyer filed the bond motion because Joe so desperately wanted it. Unfortunately the general district court judge did not believe Joe was a good risk for bond and refused to grant a bond. Joe appealed to the circuit court, but the circuit court judge also denied bond. Joe's lawyer advised him that the Court of Appeals was unlikely to grant a bond. Joe realized he'd lost his chance for freedom pending trial and decided not to have his lawyer send a written bond motion to the Court of Appeals in Richmond.

CHAPTER 5

INFORMATION ON ATTORNEY DAY

Some Virginia courts, but not all, require defendants to report who will be the defense attorney representing them if counsel is not appointed at the arraignment. In those jurisdictions, a hearing date is scheduled sometime before the preliminary hearing date. This hearing is commonly called an "information on attorney day" or "IAD." The IAD hearing is strictly a local practice in many courts throughout Virginia and is not one the law requires to happen. A court that requires an IAD hearing is not violating any constitutional rights or Virginia law.

If a lawyer enters her appearance in the case before that day, the hearing will be removed from the docket and no one will need to be present. If no attorney enters an appearance before the IAD, the accused must appear in court to explain what he has done to find a lawyer and when the accused expects to actually hire a lawyer.

Beware, failure to attend the IAD court hearing if

no lawyer has entered an appearance will result in an arrest warrant being issued for failure to appear. This is true even though courts are not required to hold IAD hearings. If local court policy requires this type of hearing, the accused must comply with the court's order.

SHEILA'S INFORMATION ON ATTORNEY HEARING

During Sheila's arraignment hearing in general district court, the judge scheduled two hearings: an "information on attorney day" and a preliminary hearing. Sheila was required to hire a lawyer before the "information on attorney day" *and* to have that lawyer enter her appearance before that day. If no attorney's name appeared in the court file on or before the "information on attorney day," Sheila would have to return to court to explain to the judge why she had not yet hired an attorney and what steps she had taken to find a lawyer.

Note: because Joe's lawyer entered her appearance quickly after the arrest, there was no need for Joe to have an "information on attorney day."

CHAPTER 6

PRELIMINARY HEARING

Preliminary hearings are usually scheduled at least six weeks after the date an accused is arrested. At a preliminary hearing the prosecution is expected to present evidence in general district court or juvenile and domestic relations court to prove to a judge that probable cause exists to believe the accused committed the crime(s) alleged. A prosecutor is not required to present the entire case against the accused. Similarly, not everyone who testifies against an accused at trial is required to testify at a preliminary hearing. The prosecutor, however, does have to present evidence regarding each element of the crime(s) at issue.

Preliminary hearings are a great way for defense attorneys to learn about the strengths and weaknesses of a case. As the prosecutor finishes asking questions of each witness, the defense attorney is allowed to ask questions of that witness through a process called cross-examination. This often gives the defense attorney more information than what could be obtained beforehand. Because the testimony is given under oath, it can be relied upon and used against the witness if the testimony changes at trial.

After hearing all of the evidence, the judge will either make a finding of probable cause and send the case to the grand jury or dismiss the charge. An accused should be hesitant to rely on the dismissal as a victory in court. A dismissal at the preliminary hearing stage of a felony case is without prejudice, meaning a prosecutor can still revive the charge by asking a grand jury for an indictment in circuit court if he believes the case is worth pursuing.

The judge is supposed to consider only the evidence that is presented in court when deciding whether to certify a case to the grand jury. However, that does not mean he has to ignore the common sense implications of what the accused says or does in court. I once had a carnal knowledge case where my client was an adult accused of having consensual sex with a teenager. Somehow, the teenage girl caught on that where the sex happened was important to the case.[15] The girl testified she couldn't remember where it happened, but it was someplace in the county. I pressed the issue in cross-examination and got her to admit it could have been outside the county. My client got very upset to hear her say that, pulled on my suit jacket, and asked me loud enough for everyone in the courtroom to hear, "How can she say that? It was special!" Needless to say, the judge believed my client really did have sex with the girl, probably in that county, and certified the case to the grand jury.

On or before the day of the preliminary hearing, a prosecutor will often make an offer for a plea agreement. Offers vary widely depending on a number of factors that may or may not be known to the defense attorney. The

---

15 Most criminal cases have to be prosecuted in the county or city where the crime happened. At the time of this preliminary hearing, the case could not go forward if the prosecutor was unable to prove the sexual encounter occurred outside the court's territory. As of July 1, 2015, the rule has changed to allow the prosecution to happen in the county where the defendant lives or where a related crime happened despite any uncertainty as to where the crime actually happened.

decision whether to accept or reject a plea offer is always one that should be made by the accused with the advice of defense counsel.

SHEILA'S PRELIMINARY HEARING

Do you remember Sheila's case? She had been charged with allowing an unauthorized person to drive (a class one misdemeanor) and possession of cocaine. Because the misdemeanor charge was unrelated to the felony, the two charges were heard separately.

The trial for allowing Joe to drive was first. Sheila decided to plead not guilty and have a trial in general district court on her first court date. During the trial, her lawyer argued that although Sheila knew after the accident that Joe had driven to work, she had not given him permission to do so and had not known he'd taken the car. The judge gave Sheila the benefit of the doubt and found her not guilty.

On the day of her preliminary hearing for

possession of cocaine, Sheila's lawyer and the prosecutor had a conversation in the hallway. The prosecutor wanted Sheila to give up her right to a preliminary hearing but was not willing to reduce the charge to a misdemeanor. The prosecutor said that if Sheila waived the hearing and pled guilty in circuit court, he would agree to recommend a first offender diversion program commonly called a 251 disposition.[16] Sheila's lawyer was not enthusiastic about the offer, but nevertheless explained it to Sheila. Sheila was terrified of having a criminal charge on her record and told her lawyer to accept the offer.

When the judge called Sheila's name, she and her lawyer went to the front of the courtroom. Sheila's lawyer explained that Sheila wished to waive her right to a preliminary hearing. The judge asked Sheila if that was correct, if she'd had enough time to discuss it with her lawyer, if the decision to waive a preliminary hearing

---

16 The diversion program is commonly called a 251 disposition in reference to Virginia Code § 18.2-251, which authorizes the program at the discretion of the trial court.

was voluntary, and if she understood what was happening. Then both Sheila and her lawyer signed the back of the cocaine arrest warrant.

The judge told Sheila the cocaine case would be sent to the grand jury for review. Sheila would have to appear in circuit court for a "term day" hearing the day after the grand jury met. Until then, she would remain free on bond.

JOE'S PRELIMINARY HEARING

On the day of Joe's preliminary hearing, the prosecutor made an offer for a plea agreement, which Joe rejected, because he firmly believed he was not guilty of anything and because he knew that his probation officer for his old drunk driving case was already trying to get Joe's suspended jail time imposed for having been arrested. Joe's lawyer explained to him that the general district court would not decide whether Joe was guilty or not guilty for any felony charge, but would only decide whether there is probable cause to allow the case to move forward to the next step in the court process.

A man named Eddie was the first witness to testify. The prosecutor asked questions first, and then Joe's lawyer had her turn. Eddie was driving on the other side of the street and saw the accident happen in his rearview mirror. Eddie described how the accident happened and mentioned he saw a man run away from the scene while Eddie was running over to offer his help. Eddie said the guy who ran away looked like Joe, but he couldn't be 100 percent certain it was actually Joe. No one person drew Eddie's attention until he saw the guy run away. The accident scene was chaotic with people yelling and crying. Other people were walking and running over to the scene at the same time Eddie was approaching. Eddie does not have personal knowledge as to whether the guy who ran away was in one of the cars or was one of the people who saw the accident happen.

The next witness to testify was Officer Smith,

who described how Joe tried to avoid being arrested by hitting him with Sheila's purse. A substance that Officer Smith believed to be cocaine fell out of the purse. Joe was promptly restrained and arrested. Officer Smith described all of Joe's statements regarding why he'd hit Officer Smith, Joe's knowledge that his license was suspended, how the accident happened, and why he left the scene of the accident. Finally, Officer Smith testified that he had been present in court on the day of Joe's first preliminary hearing and did not see Joe there. During the course of Officer's Smith's testimony, the prosecutor showed the general district court judge a copy of Joe's driving record and a certificate of analysis establishing that the powder substance was, in fact, cocaine.

The judge found Joe guilty of the misdemeanor of driving while revoked and sentenced him to serve 30 days in jail and suspended 25 days of that sentence. Then the judge certified the felony hit and run, possession of cocaine, and assaulting a police officer charges to the grand jury.

Because Joe was in jail, the judge did not want to wait for the grand jury before scheduling a trial for the felony charges. The lawyers chose a date that was after the next grand jury session and scheduled a trial in circuit court.

CHAPTER 7

GRAND JURY

A grand jury hearing is a secret proceeding. Only the prosecutor and essential witnesses attend. The grand jury listens to the evidence and votes whether to allow the case to continue to trial by issuing an indictment, which is merely an accusation. Cases reviewed by a grand jury include all felonies that have been certified after a preliminary hearing and any new charges the prosecutor wishes to begin in circuit court (a process commonly called direct indictment). Because the only evidence a grand jury hears is from the prosecution and no defense is allowed to be presented, grand juries almost always endorse the indictment as a "true bill," authorizing the case to continue to proceed. Because no defense is allowed to be presented to a grand jury, there is an old joke among attorneys that a prosecutor could indict a ham sandwich if he wanted to. In the rare case that is returned "no true bill," the prosecutor will usually drop the charge, but he can try to get an indictment from a grand jury one more time.

CHAPTER 8

TERM DAY / CIRCUIT COURT SCHEDULING HEARING

Shortly after the grand jury issues its indictments, the circuit court will hold a hearing to schedule a trial date. Some courts require the accused to attend personally so the judge can be certain the accused has actual notice of the next court date. Others ask that only the attorneys attend to avoid overcrowding in the courtroom.

The scheduling hearing is sometimes called "term day," in reference to the period in which the court is in session and in which the court expects the case to be resolved.

If the case is going to be scheduled for a trial rather than a guilty plea, the term-day judge will want to know whether a judge or jury will decide the case. Both the defendant and the prosecutor have the right to demand a jury if they want one. The only way a judge will decide the case is if both sides agree not to have a jury.

There are several factors that should be considered when deciding whether to have a jury decide the case. Judges tend to be rather jaded, because they see people try to convince them to see things their way every single day, even if it means lying to the judge. Jurors do not share that everyday experience and may be easier to persuade. If there is a jury, all 12 members of the jury must believe the defendant is guilty beyond a reasonable doubt in order for the defendant to be convicted. If even one juror has a reasonable doubt, the defendant cannot be convicted without a new trial. In some areas and types of cases, jurors may be inclined to punish defendants less harshly than judges tend to do. In other areas and types of cases (especially drug and drunk driving charges), jurors may be inclined to recommend a harsher punishment.

Perhaps the most significant factor to consider is the class level of the charge(s). Most class five and six felonies have a minimum sentence that does not include any jail time. A class four felony sentencing range includes two to 10 years of prison. A judge can suspend some or all of this time, but a jury will not be told about that possibility and cannot recommend that any time be suspended. Similarly the five- to 20-year prison sentence for a class three felony can be suspended by a judge but not by a jury. If a conviction means a lot of prison time, it may be wise to ask for a trial without a jury.

SHEILA'S TERM DAY

Term day was the day after the grand jury met and issued indictments. Sheila arrived at the courtroom about a half hour before court was supposed to start. The courtroom doors were still locked and there was already a crowd of nervous people standing in the hallway. When the courtroom was opened, the people filled the seating area to capacity. Lawyers sat in the jury seating area and did not seem as worried about their cases as the people in the benches were.

The judge came out and described the time frame

within which all cases must be scheduled for trial or for entering a guilty plea. Then he began calling the cases in alphabetical order by name of the defendants. When Sheila's name was called, she moved to the front of the courtroom and stood next to her lawyer. Sheila did not say a single word to the judge. Instead, her lawyer answered for her when her name was called and selected a date for Sheila to plead guilty. Then she was allowed to leave. The entire hearing lasted less than two minutes. Sheila left the courtroom with her lawyer, unsure of what happened. Her lawyer reassured her that the term-day hearing really was that simple and she was free to leave.

CHAPTER 9

PLEADING NOT GUILTY/TRIAL

A trial is the stage of criminal proceedings that is most often portrayed on television and in the movies. The case against the accused must be proven beyond a reasonable doubt.

A clerk will read the indictment(s) out loud. Then the accused is asked to plead guilty or not guilty to each charge separately. Once the accused has responded, the judge will ask a series of questions. How many questions are asked and what those questions are depends upon whether the plea is guilty or not guilty. The judge will ask many more questions if the accused is pleading guilty than if the accused is pleading not guilty. Either way, the judge needs to make sure the accused understands the implications of what she is doing and has made the decision whether to plead guilty or not guilty on her own without being forced into it. A good lawyer will prepare the accused before the court date to expect the questions and review the process of entering a plea.

If the plea is not guilty, the trial will begin by picking people for a jury if it is a jury trial or opening statements from the attorney if no one has requested a jury for the case. Both the prosecutor and the defense attorney will have the opportunity to present evidence and to test the strength of the other side's evidence.

The accused has the right to testify if she wants to do so. However, just like any other witness, the accused will have to swear to tell the truth. This rule is so strict that a defense lawyer who knows her client has lied while testifying is required by the ethics rules to expose the lie. Needless to say, that usually destroys all reasonable hope of a not guilty verdict.

In many cases, a good defense lawyer will advise her client not to testify. If a defendant testifies, the prosecutor will have a chance to question him on the stand. That often leaves the defendant looking much worse than he would have if he'd never testified at all.

There are some cases where there is no choice but to have the defendant testify. Sometimes there is an important fact that can't be testified about by anyone except the defendant. In many cases where there is a jury, lawyers worry about whether the jury will read something into it if the defendant does not testify. Regardless of whether the defendant chooses to testify, a good defense lawyer will be sure to inform the jury that the defense does not have to prove anything and to ask prospective jurors to accept this rule.

Most defendants are stressed out by the time their case comes to trial. They sometimes convince themselves they can correct untrue or unfair statements made during the prosecution if they just explain it all themselves, even if it means giving up the strategy they've discussed with their lawyer before trial. It's never a good idea to do this. For example, I once tried a drunk driving case without a jury in circuit court. During the police officer's testimony, my client decided he wanted to testify. I was unable to convince him it was a bad idea, and I had no choice but to let him testify. He was able to answer my questions reasonably well, even though we had not had the chance to practice testifying, but the prosecutor was able to get him to name the bar he'd gone to and several parts of the trip that had been forgotten. The prosecutor made it look like my client had blacked out, and he argued that my client obviously had an addiction to alcohol. In another case where my client was accused of assaulting a family member, my client and I had decided she would have to testify. My client was so upset to hear the family member lie in court that she chose to ignore my questions and tried to respond to the lie directly instead. Fortunately she did not sabotage her case, but she did look bad and she made it harder to win.

After all the evidence has been presented and closing arguments have concluded, the jury, or judge if there is no jury, will decide whether the accused is guilty or not guilty. A jury's decision must be unanimous and is made in a private place but announced publicly in the courtroom.

Virginia is different from most states in that the jury decides what an appropriate punishment is if it finds the accused is guilty. Therefore, the prosecutor and the defense attorney will have the opportunity to present evidence and ask the jury to consider certain evidence and even suggest a sentence within the permissible range. The jury will again deliberate in private until it comes to a unanimous decision before returning to the courtroom to announce the sentence.

Technically, the jury only recommends a sentence. The judge later imposes a sentence that does not go beyond the amount of prison time and fine recommended by the jury. However, it is extremely rare that a judge will suspend or reduce the sentence recommended by the jury, even if the jury recommends the lowest sentence it is allowed to choose. For that reason, I tell any client who is convicted by a jury to expect to serve the full sentence the jury decides is appropriate.

JOE'S NOT GUILTY PLEA AND TRIAL

Joe decided he wanted to have a trial with a jury. On the first day of his trial, the clerk read each of his charges, pausing after each one to ask Joe if he was guilty or not guilty. Joe responded that he was not guilty to all of them.

Then a lot of strangers entered the room with a deputy. The deputy read the names of 18 people. The first 14 people were assigned seats in the jury box, where jury members sit during a trial. The other four were assigned seats in the front row of the area for observers. The judge introduced himself, the lawyers, and Joe to the members of the jury. He explained why there were so many people and asked the prospective jurors some questions. Next, the prosecutor was given the opportunity to ask some questions to make sure none of the prospective jurors was biased against the government or police officers. Finally, Joe's lawyer was able to ask some questions to make sure none of the prospective jurors was biased against Joe just because he had been accused of a number of crimes.

When all of the questions were finished, the judge

explained to everyone what it is like to be a juror and how a trial works while the lawyers passed a paper back and forth to each other. The paper had a list of jurors' names, and the lawyers were taking turns scratching one name off the list until there were only 12 names remaining on the list. Those 12 people were then sworn in as jurors. Everyone who was not chosen to serve as a juror for Joe's trial was sent to the jury waiting room to learn whether they would be needed for another trial that day or excused for the rest of the day.

The jurors were given a few minutes to put personal items in the deliberation room for safekeeping and were handed a pad of paper and a pen as they returned to the courtroom. The trial began with the lawyers each explaining to the jury what the case was about. The prosecutor mentioned he would be asking the jury to find Joe guilty of drug possession, felony hit and run, driving while suspended, and assault on a police officer. Joe's lawyer asked the jury to listen closely to the evidence and require the prosecutor to prove each and every element of the crimes beyond a reasonable doubt. If they did so, they would see the prosecutor could not prove the charges and they would be asked to find Joe not guilty.

Then the prosecutor began working to prove his case by calling witnesses. First, Eddie, the eyewitness who testified at the preliminary hearing, testified about how a man ran away from the area as he approached. Eddie was shown some pictures of the accident and the other driver's body still in the car, which he confirmed were an accurate depiction of what he saw.

Then Joe's lawyer asked the witness some questions. Eddie explained he did not see how the accident occurred, but only looked in that direction after hearing a loud crash. He was too far away to see who the man was who ran away. Eddie cannot say for certain whether that person was the driver or someone else. It was a few minutes after the crashing sound before Eddie saw a man running away.

Sheila knew the prosecutor wanted her to testify about Joe having taken her car on the day of the accident and how Joe had said there'd been an accident but he was taking care of everything with the insurance company. Sheila didn't want any part of testifying against Joe and asked her lawyer to help her exercise her spousal privilege and refused to testify against Joe.[17]

Officer Smith testified about the results of his investigation and the status of Joe's license. The prosecutor submitted a copy of Joe's Virginia driving record and a certified copy of Joe's drunk driving conviction to supplement the officer's testimony. Officer Smith also testified about how Joe had hit him with Sheila's purse, dropped a small bag of cocaine powder, and tried to run

---

17 Virginia Code § 19.2-271.2 and Rule 2:504 allow a spouse to be subpoenaed to testify for the other spouse in criminal cases, but also prevent a spouse from being compelled to actually testify against the other spouse in most cases.

away when he tried to arrest Joe.

Next, Officer Smith spoke about the statements Joe made during the car ride to the adult detention center immediately after his arrest. He said Joe apologized for having hit Officer Smith and said he just did it because he was scared and didn't want to go to jail. Officer Smith described how Joe had told him why he had decided to drive to work, how the accident had happened, and that he had not asked Sheila before taking the car. When confronted with the death of the other driver, Joe was very upset and told Officer Smith the other driver was alive and Joe had called an ambulance before he ran away.

Finally, Officer Smith testified he had appeared in court on the first day scheduled for Joe's preliminary hearing, but Officer Smith did not see Joe in court that day.

During cross-examination, Officer Smith acknowledged the powder was inside the purse and Joe never said he'd known it was there. Officer Smith was not injured other than to say he felt the pressure of the purse hitting him through a bulletproof vest. Officer Smith did not seek any medical treatment as a result of this incident.

A scientist who works for the Virginia Department of Forensic Science testified that she analyzed the white powder that fell out of Sheila's purse and found it to be cocaine. She described the procedure used to analyze the substance and said she performed the test the way she was supposed to without any mistakes or distractions.

The medical examiner testified about the cause of the other driver's death. The other driver ultimately died from a massive heart attack, but sustained other significant injuries in the accident that would have quickly killed her if her heart had not given out first. During cross-examination the medical examiner admitted she could not say for certain whether the heart attack happened before or after the accident.

At the end of the medical examiner's testimony, the prosecutor told the judge he had no more witnesses. The judge asked Joe's lawyer to call her first witness. Instead, she told the judge she had a motion she would like to make outside the presence of the jury.

The judge saw that it was almost time for a break and told the jury the break would be a little longer than usual so the judge and lawyers could talk about some things. The jury was sent to the deliberation room where they could chat with each other but could not discuss the case.

When the door closed behind the last juror, Joe's lawyer asked the judge to dismiss the case against Joe for insufficient evidence. Joe's lawyer pointed out that there was no evidence Joe knew the purse contained cocaine when he used it to push Officer Smith away from him. There was also no evidence Joe knew Officer Smith was performing his duties at the time of the unfortunate encounter and that Officer Smith was not injured. Joe could not be found guilty of hit and run, because the evidence shows that someone, probably Joe, reported the accident, and because the evidence failed to prove the other driver's death was caused by the accident rather than a heart attack that occurred immediately before the accident. In fact, there was no evidence Joe caused the accident at all. Finally, Joe could not be found guilty of driving while suspended because the drunk driving conviction notes that Joe was authorized to have a restricted license upon request and the prosecutor did not prove that Joe was driving outside the terms of a restricted license. Joe could not be found guilty of failure to appear because no evidence was presented to prove that Joe had actual knowledge of the court hearing or that his absence from that hearing was willful.

The prosecutor argued he had proven the state's case and that the issues raised by Joe's lawyer were, at best, questions for the jury to consider.

The judge decided to dismiss the drug possession charge because there was no evidence that Joe knew there was cocaine in Sheila's purse until after it fell out of the purse. The other charges were allowed to be considered by the jury.

Then the judge asked if Joe's lawyer would be presenting any witnesses. Joe's lawyer said she would not be presenting any evidence, and the only thing left for Joe's lawyer to do was to present a closing argument. Finally, the judge and lawyers discussed what the jury should be instructed about the law and how it may be applied to Joe's case.

Then it was time for the jury to come back. The judge told the jury they no longer needed to consider the drug possession charge and should disregard all they had heard about cocaine. Next, the judge read to the jury all of the instructions and then allowed the lawyers to present their closing arguments.

The prosecutor spoke first, arguing that Joe had disregarded a judge's order and broken the law by driving and then made things worse by trying to run away. He ran from the accident and later punched an officer and ran away again. Then Joe ran away a third time when he failed to appear in court for his preliminary hearing. Joe is not above the law, and cannot run away from what he did, and should be found guilty.

Joe's lawyer reminded the jury how she'd asked the jury to listen very carefully to the evidence and to require the prosecutor to prove each and every element beyond a reasonable doubt. Using the jury instructions that explained what must be proven, Joe's lawyer repeated the same arguments she'd made to the judge.

The prosecutor had the last chance to speak to the jury and stressed it did not matter who caused the accident or that Joe had called 911. The fact was that Joe had driven when he wasn't supposed to. Instead of staying to report the accident to the police like he was supposed to, he ran away from the scene of a car accident in which an innocent person had died. Then Joe tried to run away a second time by violently punching Officer Smith with a purse and yet again when he skipped court. That means Joe is guilty of the crimes and the jury should come back with a guilty verdict for all of the charges.

The jury spent the rest of the day and three hours on the next day discussing the case in the deliberation room in secret. Because Joe was an inmate, he was not allowed to wait inside the courtroom with his lawyer and his family there to support him. Instead, Joe had to wait in a nearby jail cell. Joe thought he would go crazy sitting in that cell by himself with nothing to do while a group of 12 strangers were in the next room deciding his fate, but somehow he got through it.

Finally, one of the jurors knocked on the door and told the deputy they had reached a verdict. Everyone was called back into the room before the jury was allowed to enter. When the jury came in, the judge asked the foreman to read the verdict. The jury found Joe guilty of felony hit and run, not guilty of driving while suspended, guilty of assaulting a police officer, and not guilty of failure to appear in court. The judge asked each juror if he or she agreed with the verdict and each one responded, "Yes."

The judge then told the jury they would have to

decide what sentence should be imposed for the hit and run and for assaulting a police officer. When the judge finished instructing the jury about the permissible sentencing range, the prosecutor asked the jury to give the defendant a lot of jail time, and Joe's lawyer asked for six months (the minimum jail sentence allowed). The jury returned to the deliberation room to discuss sentencing.

After two more hours of deliberation, the jury came to an agreement. The jury recommended a sentence of six months in jail and a $2,500 fine for hit and run. The recommended sentence for assaulting a police officer was two years in prison and an additional $2,500 fine. The judge thanked the jury for their service and sent the jurors to the jury waiting room before going home.

Joe's lawyer asked the judge to set aside both the verdict and the sentence, arguing the jury was obviously unreasonable. The judge disagreed and ordered a probation officer to complete an investigation of Joe's life, prepare sentencing guidelines for the judge to consider, and recommend an appropriate sentence. A sentencing hearing was scheduled for a Friday morning three months later. The trial was now over, and Joe went back to jail to wait for his sentencing hearing.

CHAPTER 10

PLEADING GUILTY

In many cases a defendant will plead guilty. This most often happens when a defense attorney's investigation reveals the defendant is likely to be convicted if she has a trial and when the attorney is able to negotiate a reasonable plea agreement with the prosecutor. In some cases the defendant may choose to plead guilty without any agreement with the prosecutor.

A guilty plea begins in the same way as a not guilty plea. A clerk will read the indictment(s)[18] out loud. Then the accused is asked to plead guilty or not guilty to each charge separately. Once the accused has responded, the judge will ask a series of questions. This interaction between the judge and defendant is called a plea colloquy.

---

18 An indictment is the legal term for the document that accuses someone of a crime when the trial for that crime is in circuit court. General district courts and juvenile and domestic relations courts do not use indictments.

When a defendant pleads guilty, he is asked more questions than when he pleads not guilty. The defendant's lawyer should prepare him to answer those questions in advance of the guilty plea hearing.

SHEILA PLEADS GUILTY

Sheila met with her lawyer a few days before the court hearing where she was going to plead guilty. Her lawyer explained to her that Virginia has discretionary sentencing guidelines, which judges usually follow but are free not to follow. The guidelines take into consideration the severity of the crime, including anything that makes Sheila's crime worse than other possession cases, and Sheila's criminal record. Sheila had never been convicted of any crimes ever before in her life and did not have any aggravating factors for the judge to take into consideration. As a result, the guidelines in her case recommended that she be ordered into probation and not sentenced to jail at this time.

Next, Sheila's lawyer described a diversion program for first offenders, commonly called a 251 disposition.

The judge could decide to accept Sheila's guilty plea but postpone the decision to convict her for about two years. Sheila would have to complete 24 hours of community service and a drug education program, which would be supervised by a probation officer. Her driver's license would also be suspended for six months, but she could have a restricted license, which would allow her to drive to work, church, the doctor, court, drug classes, and the probation office. Finally, Sheila would have to pay all the court costs associated with her case. If she successfully completes the program and does not get any new charges, the case will be dismissed. [19] It would appear on her criminal record as a dismissal but would never be eligible for expungement if Sheila were to later decide she wanted to erase it off her record. Her lawyer believed she would be an excellent candidate for the diversion program.

---

19 Although this type of program results in a dismissal, it is sometimes treated as a conviction, most notably by immigration officials. You should always discuss the pros and cons of this type of arrangement with your lawyer before enrolling in the diversion program.

After Sheila and her lawyer were finished discussing the possibilities of what the judge will decide to do to her, they discussed what it is like to plead guilty to a felony in circuit court. Most importantly, her lawyer told her to keep calm and listen to everything she was asked during the hearing.

On the day of Sheila's hearing, the judge's clerk read the indictment for possession of cocaine out loud and asked if she pled guilty or not guilty. Sheila was standing next to her lawyer while this was happening and responded "guilty." Next, the clerk asked Sheila to raise her right hand and swear to answer some questions truthfully. Then the judge began to ask Sheila many "yes or no" questions. After she answered all of the questions, the judge told Sheila that she and her lawyer could sit down. Then the judge asked the prosecutor to describe the incident that led to Sheila's arrest. Instead of having witnesses testify, the prosecutor told the judge a summary of what the case was about. When he was done, Sheila's lawyer said she did not have anything to add to the prosecutor's description. The judge found Sheila guilty of possession of cocaine.

The last few minutes of Sheila's hearing were dedicated to choosing a date for a sentencing hearing. Then the prosecutor asked the judge to revoke Sheila's bond and make her wait for her sentencing hearing in a jail cell. Sheila's lawyer objected and pointed out to the judge that Sheila has never missed a hearing or even arrived late. Furthermore, her guidelines recommend probation and no jail. There is no reason to believe Sheila will not come to court or that she is a danger to the community. The judge denied the prosecutor's motion to revoke bond and allowed her to remain out of jail until the sentencing hearing.

The judge told Sheila she would have to meet with a probation officer and cooperate in an investigation of her background for the purpose of preparing a pre-sentence report. As part of that process, Sheila would be required to submit to random drug testing at the probation officer's discretion. The judge also told Sheila she was forbidden to drink alcohol from now on as a new condition of her bond. Finally, Sheila was told she must return to court three months later with her lawyer for a sentencing hearing.

CHAPTER 11

PRE-SENTENCE INVESTIGATION AND REPORT

In most cases where an accused has been found guilty of a felony, the judge will not impose a sentence right away. Instead, she will schedule a sentencing hearing on another day and order that a probation officer conduct an investigation of the convicted person's life history and criminal history for the judge to take into consideration.

The probation officer's report will include information about both the state's and the accused's version of the events leading up to the arrest, as well as the accused's academic career, social history, employment history, and criminal record. The probation officer will also write a recommendation as to what an appropriate sentence would be using the Virginia Sentencing Guidelines. A copy of the report with the sentencing guidelines is given to the judge, the prosecutor, and the defense attorney for review prior to the sentencing hearing.

SHEILA'S PRE-SENTENCE
INVESTIGATION AND REPORT

Immediately after the hearing ended where Sheila pled guilty, she went to visit the local Department of Corrections probation office to make arrangements to participate in an investigation of her background. The probation officer was too busy to interview her at that time and scheduled an appointment for her to come back on another day.

When Sheila went for her appointment, she was asked to explain her side of the story about what happened. Sheila explained she was a cocaine addict at the time of the offense but has been in treatment for her addiction since she was arrested. She had some cocaine in her purse. Joe picked up Sheila's purse and accidentally dropped it on the ground, which caused it to break open. A police officer who was standing nearby saw the cocaine fall onto the ground and arrested her for having it.

Sheila answered many questions about her childhood, her education, her family, her work history, her criminal record, and her history of drug addiction. After she was finished answering questions, she took a drug test and went home.

In the days that followed, the probation officer verified the information that could be verified. He also reviewed her criminal record and asked the prosecutor to provide the official state version of the facts. He compared Sheila's criminal record and the official state version of what happened to trigger the arrest with Virginia's Sentencing Guidelines. Then he wrote a report, which included all of the information he received from both Sheila and the prosecutor, the results of the drug test, Sheila's criminal record, the sentencing guidelines, and a formal recommendation that Sheila be ordered into active probation. The report further noted that Sheila was eligible to participate in a diversion program commonly called a 251 disposition, which would result in her case being dismissed if she could comply with all of the rules of the program.

After the report was prepared, Sheila met with her lawyer to review every line on every page to make sure all of the information was correct. Sheila was nervous going to the appointment, but her lawyer told her up front that the probation officer was recommending either the diversion program or probation and Sheila was not likely to be going to jail after the sentencing hearing. When she heard that, Sheila was able to relax a little and review the report with her lawyer.

Sheila believed all of the information she provided was accurately represented in the report. She acknowledged that her version of the incident was a little different from the prosecutor's version, but her lawyer assured her the differences were not significant and were unlikely to create a problem for her.

JOE'S PRE-SENTENCE INVESTIGATION AND REPORT

After Joe's trial, his lawyer came to visit him at the jail and told him a probation officer would be coming to visit him. The probation officer would want a lot of information about Joe's background, education, family, drug and alcohol use, and his version of what happened. Anything Joe said about the hit and run or the assault charge would be considered an admission and could ruin his chance for an appeal; therefore, Joe should tell the probation officer his lawyer advised him not to say anything about what happened and refuse to write his version of what happened.

As in Sheila's case, the probation officer verified the information that could be verified. He also reviewed Joe's criminal record and asked the prosecutor to provide the official state version of the facts. He used Joe's criminal record and the official state version of what happened to trigger the arrest to calculate Virginia's Sentencing Guidelines. Then he wrote a report, which included all of the information he received from both Joe and the prosecutor,

Joe's criminal record, the sentencing guidelines, and a formal recommendation that Joe be given the sentence recommended by the jury, and he noted that six months of the prison time is a mandatory minimum sentence required by law.

CHAPTER 12

SENTENCING

The final stage of a felony trial is the sentencing hearing. At this time the prosecutor and defense attorney will have one last chance to present evidence and argument about an appropriate sentence. The now-convicted person will also have an opportunity to speak before the judge announces what the sentence will be.

Not all cases result in years in prison, but most do carry some period of active probation, even if no active jail or prison time is ordered. Most felony sentences include a suspended period of incarceration. A suspended sentence means the time is not served in the beginning, but if there are any probation violations or new convictions, the suspended sentence may be imposed in addition to any other penalties the accused may be facing. All felony convictions require the accused to pay court costs in addition to any fines or restitution payments that may be ordered. Likewise, everyone convicted of a felony is required to submit a sample of DNA for entry into a database. Additional penalties may be ordered at sentencing and may be required by law depending upon the nature of the charge.

In cases where a sentence has been recommended by a jury, the judge cannot impose any fines or jail time that exceed the jury's recommendation. The judge can legally reduce or suspend part of the jury's recommended sentence, but it is very unlikely he will do so absent some unusual circumstances.

In cases where the defendant either pled guilty or was found guilty after a trial without a jury, the judge has several choices. Common possibilities include active jail or prison time, a period of suspended incarceration, restitution, a fine, suspension of the defendant's driver's license, community service, and probation.

A. ACTIVE JAIL/PRISON SENTENCE

Many felony sentences include a period of incarceration either at the local adult detention center or in the state prison system. If the prisoner obeys the rules and does not get in any trouble with prison officials, she will get credit for having spent more time in prison than she was there in real life. This extra credit is commonly referred to as good time or good time credit. Felony convictions may earn good time credit for any time served after the sentencing hearing, but the defendant will have to serve at least 85 percent of the time ordered by the judge. Any mandatory minimum sentence must be served in its entirety without any good time credit towards an early release date.

Although this book does not go into detail about misdemeanors, the reader may be interested to know how misdemeanor time is credited as being served. People who are convicted of misdemeanors are eligible to receive good time credit at the rate of two days credit for every day served that is not part of a mandatory minimum. For most misdemeanors, this means the defendant will be required to serve only one-half of the time ordered, assuming she obeys the rules of the jail.

The Department of Corrections will determine an expected release date shortly after the sentencing hearing and inform the inmate of when that date is. If the inmate is transferred to a state prison, the information will be available online through the Virginia Department of Corrections' offender locator at http://vadoc.virginia.gov/offenders/locator/. If the inmate stays in a local jail, the records department of some jails will advise any interested person who calls of the anticipated release date.

B. SUSPENDED JAIL/PRISON TIME

Suspended jail time is a jail or prison sentence that is not required to be served immediately. It is used to motivate the defendant to obey the rules of probation and any program that he may be ordered to complete. It is also used to encourage the defendant to avoid any behavior that could lead him to commit new crimes. If the defendant breaks the probation rules or if he is convicted of a new crime (date of offense occurring after the date of the sentencing hearing), he will have to return to court and face the possibility of having to serve some or all of the time that had previously been suspended. A sentence for a probation violation is in addition to any sentence that may be imposed for a new charge.

C. RESTITUTION

The Virginia Constitution's Bill of Rights guarantees the right of victims of a crime to be reimbursed for any financial loss incurred as the direct result of a crime. This issue arises most often in embezzlement and destruction of property cases but can be an issue in other cases as well.

D. FINES / COURT COSTS

Like a jail sentence, any fine ordered by a judge can be suspended either partially or in its entirety. Not all felony and misdemeanor sentences include a fine. However, juries often include a fine in their sentencing recommendations. If a jury recommends a fine, a defendant can expect it to be imposed even if there is also a jail sentence.

Anyone who is convicted of a felony, misdemeanor,

or traffic infraction must pay the court costs associated with their case. The amount of court costs varies depending on a number of circumstances. A felony that is reduced to a misdemeanor in general district court or juvenile and domestic relations court without ever going to circuit court does not get billed circuit court fees. A jury trial increases court costs. A defendant who has a court-appointed attorney (public defender) is also expected to reimburse the court for attorney's fees if he is convicted. These are just a few of the variables that determine the dollar amount of court costs. The best way to determine the amount of court costs is to ask the clerk when making arrangements to pay the fine.

Court costs for felony cases that are resolved by a jury trial can be very, very expensive, even more if the trial result is appealed to the Court of Appeals and affirmed. Virginia law allows up to 30 days to pay a fine and court costs in full without any extra penalty. If a defendant needs more time to pay, she can request an extended deadline or a payment plan.[20] Court policy on this subject varies among different courts. If a defendant believes she will need time to pay, she or her lawyer should look into the local court practices to be sure to get the extension or payment plan without trouble.

If the fine and court costs are not paid in full on time, the Virginia Department of Motor Vehicles will automatically suspend the defendant's privilege to drive in Virginia, even if the person has never had a license. The state will also automatically add a 17 percent penalty to the unpaid balance 40 days after the sentencing hearing (or the defendant's release from incarceration). Unpaid fines and court costs also accrue interest if they are not paid in a timely manner.[21]

Another option for people without funds to pay off their fines and court costs is to participate in a community

---

20 Virginia Code § 19.2-354.
21 Virginia Code § 19.2-353.5.

service program supervised by the local sheriff's department.[22] Virginia law requires every court to have such a program. The convicted defendant will earn credit towards his fines and court costs on an hourly basis. If the defendant does not appear for work on time or does not comply with the rules of the program, he can be removed from the work program and prevented from re-enrolling in the program.

E. SUSPENSION OF DRIVER'S LICENSE

Most felony charges do not include a license suspension as part of their sentencing structure. The most notable exceptions include all drug possession and distribution offenses, leaving the scene of an accident, and driving while intoxicated.

---

22 Virginia Code § 19.2-354.

F. COMMUNITY SERVICE

Felony sentences do not often include community service, even though many defendants ask their lawyer to try to arrange for community service instead of jail or prison. It is not impossible for a judge to order community service, just very unlikely unless it is part of a deferred disposition.[23]

The most common type of case that includes community service in the sentence is a first-offense drug possession. In those cases, Virginia law allows the judge to postpone the sentencing hearing and ultimately dismiss the case if the defendant completes 24 hours of community service, successfully completes a drug program, pays the court costs, and accepts a six-month suspension of his

---

23 A deferred disposition is an order to do certain things in order to have a charge dismissed. The most common example in a felony case happens in first-offense drug possession cases. In those cases, a judge may dismiss the charge if the defendant does community service, goes to a drug program, has his driver's license suspended, and successfully participates in probation.

driver's license. A defendant in this diversion program can be granted a restricted license to drive for very limited purposes.

G. POST-RELEASE SUPERVISION / PROBATION

Most felony sentences include a period of probation for defendants who are not incarcerated or post-release supervision for people who serve a jail or prison sentence. Both programs require the defendant to meet with a probation officer on a regular basis. The appointment schedule is determined by the probation officer and can be adjusted as the probation officer deems appropriate.

The probation officer will require the defendant to obey a number of rules. Most of the rules are generally required of all probationers. Examples of these rules include random drug testing, avoiding criminal activity, reporting any police contact to the probation officer, earning a GED if the defendant has not graduated high school, and learning English if the defendant does not speak English.

Most judges will also order the defendant to seek and maintain full-time employment, even though many defendants report being unable to find a job after being convicted of a felony. As a practical matter, looking for a job and not getting one will not normally trigger a probation violation hearing; but not looking for one, getting fired for cause, or not making payments towards restitution, fines, court costs, or other case-related fees may cause a probation officer to schedule a violation hearing in court.

Some rules may be specifically required by a judge in certain cases. Examples of this type of rule include timely restitution payments, community service hours, an anger management program, and no contact with the victim of a crime. The probation officer can also impose additional requirements on a defendant if the defendant needs help with drug addiction or is breaking minor rules that can be addressed without asking a judge to impose the suspended sentence.

SHEILA'S SENTENCING HEARING

At Sheila's sentencing hearing, both the prosecutor and Sheila's lawyer agreed she was eligible for a 251 disposition diversion program. The prosecutor did not object to Sheila being given the opportunity to avoid a conviction and participate in the program.

The judge vacated[24] the conviction he'd entered on the day Sheila pled guilty and postponed the sentencing hearing for two years. In the meantime, Sheila would have to do certain things:

1. She would be placed on active probation for the whole two years. This means she would have to meet with a probation officer whenever the probation officer wanted her to come to the office. She could also have telephone appointments with the probation officer in addition to the

---

24 To say the judge "vacated" the conviction means he undid it or legally erased it.

live appointments. She would have to obey all rules of the probation office.

2. She would have to participate in a drug education program and whatever additional drug treatment the probation officer believed appropriate. This would include random drug screens throughout the entire two years she was going to be on probation.

3. She would have to complete 24 hours of community service, which could be performed at any legitimate charity and which would be supervised by her probation officer.

4. Sheila's driver's license was suspended for six months. However, the judge considered and granted Sheila's request for a restricted license. While her license was suspended, Sheila would be allowed to drive to and from work, the doctor, church, probation, the drug program, and court only during the times she normally drives to those places. If she drove even five minutes outside of that time frame, she could be arrested for driving while suspended

and would be deemed to have violated the terms of her probation, meaning she would be convicted of felony drug possession in addition to driving while suspended.

5. She could not have any new criminal behavior while she was on probation. If she did get a new conviction, she would be convicted and sentenced on both the felony drug possession and the new charge.

Before Sheila was allowed to leave the courtroom, the judge told her she was being given a huge break. If she does not do everything she is supposed to do, she would likely be facing not only a felony conviction, but jail or prison time for disobeying the court's orders. Sheila promised she would do everything the judge ordered and went straight to the probation office to begin working with her probation officer.

SHEILA'S PROBATION AND
FINAL CASE OUTCOME

While Sheila's case was pending, she had many sleepless nights and stress-filled crying spells wondering what was going to happen to her. She felt very lucky to have gotten into a diversion program and was determined not to blow it. While she was on probation, she did not use alcohol, cocaine, or any other drug. She never missed a single appointment with her probation officer or drug education class.

She found she enjoyed doing community service, because it made her feel good to help people who were less fortunate than herself, and it aided in her personal recovery from addiction. She continued doing service hours throughout the entire two-year probation period, even after she finished the hours she'd been ordered to do, and got an excellent evaluation from the supervisor.

When the two years were over, Sheila reported back to court and had a final sentencing hearing in front of the same judge who had allowed her to do the program. The judge mentioned how pleased he was with Sheila's excellent behavior while in the program and dismissed Sheila's felony drug possession charge.

Sheila's lawyer reminded her she did not qualify to have the charge removed from her criminal record through the expungement process, but her record also would not show a conviction. Sheila was not worried, because she had already been living with that status for two years and learned things were not as bad as she had feared before she started the diversion program.

JOE'S SENTENCING HEARING

A few days before Joe's sentencing hearing, his lawyer went to visit him at the jail and brought a copy of the pre-sentence report with her. They reviewed all of the information in the report to make sure it was correct. Then they discussed the likely sentence Joe would be receiving.

Joe's lawyer explained that he would likely be serving a felony sentence that totaled two years and six months and $5,000 in fines in addition to court costs.

Joe's driver's license would probably be suspended for six months. Upon his release from prison, he would have to participate in a form of active probation called post-release supervision, which would have additional suspended jail time built into the sentence. Even though the judge could suspend part of the jury's sentence, he was very unlikely to do so, because the jury's recommendation is given very serious consideration as the voice of the community.

On the day of the sentencing hearing, the prosecutor and Joe's lawyer were given the opportunity to make corrections, additions, and/or deletions to the sentencing report and ask the probation officer questions about it. Both lawyers were asked if they wanted to present additional evidence, and both lawyers said no. Then both lawyers were allowed to tell the judge what they wanted the sentence to be and why the judge should agree.

After the lawyers were done speaking, the judge asked if there was any reason why a sentence should not be imposed that day. There was no reason. Then the judge asked Joe if he wanted to say anything before the sentence was imposed. Joe said no and looked down at the table while he nervously waited to hear his fate.

The judge announced Joe's sentence for assaulting a police officer first: two years in prison and a $2,500 fine. Then the judge sentenced Joe to an additional six months in jail and a $2,500 fine for hit and run. The judge suspended Joe's driver's license for six months and ordered Joe to pay the costs associated with the court case, participate in two years of post-trial supervision upon his release from prison, submit a sample of his DNA to the state's database of convicted felons, seek and maintain full-time employment upon his release from prison, complete a substance abuse evaluation and comply with any recommendations for treatment, and remain of uniform good behavior with no further violations of law while he is in post-release supervision.

The judge wished Joe luck in the future and dismissed Joe to serve his sentence. Joe was escorted back to the jail to wait for a transfer to the state prison system where he would serve the balance of his jail sentence.

EPILOGUE

A NOTE ABOUT COLLATERAL CONSEQUENCES

Criminal defendants often ask just as many questions about what life will be like when the court case is over as they do about what will happen in court. The purpose of this book is not to predict the future of any criminal defendant, but it would be incomplete if some of the common consequences of a felony conviction were not described here.

1. CIVIL RIGHTS ARE FORFEITED

These rights include the right to vote, the right to serve on a jury, and the right to serve as a notary public. A convicted felon may petition the Virginia governor for restoration of these rights. At the time of this writing, the process is relatively simple and does not require help from an attorney. More information about reinstating civil rights can be found online at https://commonwealth.virginia.gov/ judicial-system/restoration-of-rights/.

2. THE RIGHT TO BEAR ARMS IS FORFEITED

Convicted felons are not allowed to possess any firearm, not even people who like to hunt. It does not matter whether the felony conviction was for a violent crime or a nonviolent crime. If a person who has been convicted of a felony is found in possession of a firearm without having his right to possess a firearm restored in Virginia, he can expect to be convicted of a new felony and spend some time in prison.[25]

The right to possess a firearm in Virginia can be restored by a Virginia circuit court only after the convicted felon has had his civil rights restored by the governor.[26] It is important to note the circuit court can only restore the

---

25 Virginia Code § 18.2-308.2(A).
26 Virginia Code § 18.2-308(C).

right to *possess* a firearm and does not on its face include the right to buy and sell firearms or transport them across state lines. A convicted felon who wishes to possess a firearm outside of Virginia should verify that state's laws before attempting to do so or risk a prison sentence in the other state. Federal law does not presently provide a way for convicted felons to regain their firearm rights.

3. IMMIGRANTS CAN BE REMOVED FROM THE UNITED STATES

Immigration law provides for removal (commonly called deportation) of most immigrants who are convicted of an aggravated felony. All Virginia felonies are considered to be "aggravated" for immigration purposes and can result in deportation. If the felony involves drugs, a weapon, or moral turpitude (generally meaning crimes that include lying, cheating, or stealing), it will be even harder to avoid getting deported or removed from the United States. This means some convictions can trigger deportation proceedings for multiple reasons.

4. CONVICTED FELONS ARE DISQUALIFIED FROM STUDENT LOANS AND PUBLIC ASSISTANCE

The federal regulations do not authorize student loans, housing assistance, or other public benefits that are meant to offer help to people in financial need.

5. PROFESSIONAL LICENSES AND BUSINESS LICENSES MAY BE FORFEITED

A person whose profession requires a license such as a lawyer, doctor, nurse, masseuse, or an accountant, and who has been convicted of a felony may face license revocation proceedings from the organization that supervises people of that profession.

6. POTENTIAL EMPLOYERS MAY REFUSE TO HIRE CONVICTED FELONS

Many convicted felons complain they cannot get a job of any kind due to the mistakes of their past. A felony conviction often makes life harder in the beginning, but can get somewhat easier as the years pass without new charges. Some convicted felons are fortunate to find a job that pays a living wage. Some are not able to do so. Others find a way to earn money by running their own business.

People who have been convicted of one or more felonies may face other adversities in life. It is impossible to predict how any individual or private agency will respond to the discovery of a felony conviction in a person's past. As with all adversities in life, it is up to the individual to find a way to overcome her past and begin a new life as a law-abiding citizen.

ABOUT THE AUTHOR

Jennifer Raimo has been fascinated by criminal justice ever since she picked up her first Nancy Drew book in the fourth grade. As a criminal justice major, she volunteered with an outreach group from St. Francis College in Loretto, Pennsylvania to plan special events such as holiday celebrations and movie nights for teens in jail. Her criminal justice experience since college includes work as a corrections officer in Pennsylvania and other religious volunteer work at a juvenile detention center in New York.

Jennifer Raimo graduated from George Mason Law School in 2001. Having passed three state bar exams on the first try, two of which were in the same week, her friends and family enjoy challenging her to collect all 50 state bars. She currently practices criminal law in northern Virginia, where she has worked as a sole practitioner since 2012.

WA